Love Sober

An Anthology of 20 years of Poetry

Steven McCombs

ISBN: 9798628402504

Cover design by: Art Painter
Library of Congress Control Number: 2018675309
Printed in the United States of America

Contents

Introduction

This book of poems will not be for everyone, though I do hope everyone that does read it enjoys it. At times it can be dark and at time it can be joyous. The majority of these poems are about love, both the ups and downs, good and bad. A few other poems are in here as well as this collection encompasses every poem or song I've written in nearly 20 years. If you want more details about a certain poem, feel free to drop me an email at Steven.Mccombs77@gmail.com

This book of poems will not be for everyone, though I do hope everyone that does read it enjoys it. At times it can be dark and at time it can be joyous. The majority of these poems are about love both the ups and downs, good and bad. A few other poems are in there as well as this collection encompasses every poem or song I've written in nearly 20 years. If you want more details about a certain poem, feel free to drop me an email at Steven.Mccombs77@gmail.com

A Golden Treasure

A warm glow;
a gentle flow.
My heart has been stolen;
by a treasure I consider golden.
Someone I just want to hold through the night;
and tell her everything's going to be alright.
The first love of my life;
hopefully someday my wife.
To love and to cherish;
through sickness and through health.
I wish I may, I wish I might;
I wish I was with her tonight.

A Lovers Poem

Beautiful fire red lips,
and those narrow hips.
Sparkling bright eyes,
not enough hellos and too many good byes.
Shimmering hair, radiant even in the night,
tell me everything will be alright.
My heart is on fire this night,
it won't go out without a fight.
An emptiness fills me when she's not around,
but I've always told myself to be proud.
A feeling I've never felt before,
the feeling for the heart to soar.
I feel alone when I can't see her,
I would die just be near her.

Misty's Poem

I'm glad we're still friends,
Even though I'll always think of you as something more.
I hope our relation can grow back to what it once was.
God, I hope so.
I try to never break a promise,
So these things we still have to do:
For your birthday if think,
Since if have no idea what to get you,
Maybe a movie
Involving some strange talking vegetables
That you always wanted to view.
If you so desire,
I would still like to attend the next dance with you,
Preferably, more than just friends,
But if that's all it can be,
Then if guess it'll have to do.
And I'm still going to go,
And see you do all your cheers.
At least so if can say
"She was once mine,
And in my heart,
She always will be."

Candy Eyed Lids

I play games with my mind,
while she plays game with my heart.
I dream about her,
while she cut's through my veins.
My heart bleeds for her.
My blood flows.
They say,
'Birds of a feather,
Flock together'
But I have lost my wings.
Like I have lost her.
Tensing and Teasing,
Yearning and Pleasing,
Her lips once lay upon mine.
Desire and ecstasy,
she used to bring to me.
But now I am alone.
Without her,
I know only suffering.
I feel only pain.
I see her lips in my mind,
pressed against mine.

Come Back Love

Every time I see you my day gets brighter;
You are my heart, my soul, my burning fire.
When I think of you my heart soars above the night's sky;
Then I sit and wonder why? Why? Why?
I love the way you laugh,
The way you make me smile;
Then I think about our times
How they were all worthwhile.
I came today to say how much I care;
To tell you how much I wish you were here.

Confusion

What did I do to deserve this?
We never even got to kiss.
Now I'm alone;
My heart is not prone;
To the damage dealt to it;
It doesn't have the sharpest wit.
If I could have just one more chance;
Maybe to get in that first dance.
Your friend deceived thee;
Jealously because you are with me.
My heart will never waver;
You will always be its favor.
If anyone tells you otherwise;
It's nothing but a collection of lies;
At home or away;
My heart will never stray.

Day Dreaming

Walking down the dark damp hall;
Trying not to stumble and fall;
I turn on the lights;
The birds take flight.
Soothing scents of lavender and cream;
This all seems like a dream.
As sweet as a kiss;
A taste of eternal bliss.
I wait in pain;
I wait in vain.
I strive, and I strive, will this moment ever arrive?
It is now dawn;
I find myself on the front lawn.
I wish it were December;
And I hope you remember;
Our gentle kiss;
Eternal bliss.

Day Six

And so I go on,
Not finding my dreams.
If I close my eyes,
Nightmares will awake.
My strength is failing me,
What little I have left.
Please just end my misery,
It would all be better that way.

Drive

I stare into the night;
Never turning on a light;
I drive and I drive,
And eventually I arrive;
On the corner of 5th street on Heavenly drive;
I hear a sound;
Suddenly I turn around;
I see to my amazement;
A pillow and a mint;
It was all just a dream;
Good thing I didn't scream;
But wait, there's more;
Ever after, nevermore.

Drown Me

Let these rivers wash away my tears.
Being alone is my biggest fear.
I never knew love before,
But now I can't let it go.
Holding on to her,
Is so hard to do,
When she pushes me away,
Off into the waves.
I don't know what to do.
I want her back,
But I don't know how.
Let these waves drown me,
So at least if don't have to see.
The only thing if want,
Is for me to be with her.
The only thing that won't be.
Not because of her,
But because of me.
Please drown me.

Eternal Fire

My heart's on fire,
You're its one desire.
Tangled web of confusion,
It's no illusion.
Struck by cupids arrow,
As swift as a sparrow.
No matter what I say,
I hope you'll stay.
I'll always love you,
I hope you'll love me too.
Love struck,
Or maybe just by dumb luck.
Forever burning,
Twisting and turning,
Yearning and yearning,
You never quit learning.
As beautiful as a dove,
Is it me you love?
A desire to see thee,
Underneath the mistletoe tree.
You're my hearts one desire, its eternal fire

Failure Prevailing

I would shed a tear for my love,
as I would shed my live for her,
Beheld with the beauty of a dove,
She is the one I love.
But some things will never be.
I guess those some things are me?
I wish things could be,
But she doesn't agree.
I've become,
A failure.
In my own eyes,
I can't succeed.

Fool

She's a cold-hearted fool,
Who's lost the only one who's ever truly,
Loved her.
She'll never find love again.
It's left her,
Turn-tailed and ran,
Wanting to get away from her.
Cold attacks of false-fiction,
Love laughs at the despair.
For he will never go back to her,
Not now,
Not ever.
Whether or not she wants him.
He knows too well,
Knows better now,
Then to step blind-folded into the future.
To learn from the past.
The only true history lesson ever learned

Forever Lost

I don't want to feel this way
Don't want to feel the walls around me.
Burning in eternal damnation.
Repent thy sins they call out
Well screw them!
They don't know better!
Puppets of a greater scheme!
They are a fool's paradox,
The laughing stock of my imagination.
The voices scream out loud,
Vile sounds of loathing death surround me,
I have been engulfed by rages blind fury.
When will I find my way out of this wretch?

Forget About it

Walking down the aisle;
I see her,
All I can do is smile;
The time is right;
But everything seems so wrong;
What did I expect?
Maybe a hug and a kiss?
The taste of bliss on the lips?
I was a fool;
She doesn't love me at all;
I had my chance;
But that all in the past;
If only again;
Things would be different

I am alone

Darkness invades my mind.
Light grows harder to find.
Misery marches over my spine.
Contempt for what isn't mine.
This Feeling of hatred is misleading.
Days have gone by of me bleeding,
From the insides of my soul I bleed.
From theses nightmares I have I scream.
Impure thoughts overcome me of treachery.
I have committed grave debauchery.
These feelings I have are misleading.
Days have gone by without me sleeping
I write this dark poetry,
Depressing me over what can never be.
I sing my melancholy melodies,
Depressing me over what I once thought
Would be.

I Dream

I dream of life, never ending.
I dream of death, always there.
I dream of fire, forever burning.
I dream of water, never cooling.
I dream of peace, a world of harmony.
I dream of war, a world of hate.
I dream hope, and all that is sacred.
I dream of despair, the feeling of being
Scared.
I dream of happiness, and that which could
Be.
I dream of sorrow, a feeling all too familiar
To me.
I dream of love, between you and me.
I dream of you, and the way things used to
Be.

Lost

Lost in a maze of undesirable truths;
You find things you don't want know;
Love seems like a lie;
A lie you can't live without;
What has happened to me?
I used to be strong?
I used to be smart?
I never said anything wrong?
What has love done to me?
Angry and confused,
Tears of frustration fall from me;
I wish they'd drown me.
Rose petals of razors;
The white dove is now the crow;
The flowers are wilting;
I don't know what to do.

Love?

I lie her and wait for an answer;
the most important question any man can ask;
does she love me?
A question that can never be answered by one's words;
But only by one's heart.
The answer bewilders me;
Because of my desire to be with thee;
I don't think she'll ever understand;
what it's like to be me;
I love her with all my heart;
But does she love me?
Does she care?
thorns of a rose pierce my heart;
The bleedings just begun to start;
Ruby waterfalls flowing swiftly;
The heart withholds ever so gallantly;
trying to hold onto the rope;
To not fall, and slide down the slope

Meeting Someone New

Met someone new,
Earlier on this year.
The first day I met her,
Away my heart flew
She was so beautiful to me,
With short auburn brown hair,
Sweetest thing I ever have seen.
I couldn't help but to stare.
Her pretty eyes and gorgeous smile,
Make the end of my day all worthwhile.
I'd give so much to be with her.
Give her my heart, my soul,
I'd even give up my life to be with her,
If that's what it took.
I dream of us together at beautiful sites.
Walking along beaches,
Holding each other's hands,
The sun just coming into view,
As we're playing like little kids in the
Sand.

Meeting Someone New Two

I know chances are it will never be,
But that doesn't take away my hopes and
Dreams.
I'll always have hope,
For as long as I can,
For who knows,
Maybe someday,
My dreams will come into play.
And I'll live my life my way.
As it was always meant to be.

Midnight Roaming

Thursday night;
No one's in sight;
An hour long stroll;
Forever searching for one's soul;
A long road to one's heart;
It's hard to see from end to start;

My Sleeping Angel

My sleeping angel lies there quietly,
Smiling ever so slightly.
She's so precious to me,
Most beautiful thing I have ever seen.
I would give up everything just to have her
Gentle embrace.
I would hold her, and she would hold me.
And we could meet every day, hopefully,
Underneath our very own private mistletoe tree.
My sleeping angel, if desire to be with thee,
But I guess certain things aren't meant to
Be.

She Flew Away

Every day she goes farther away,
Yet everyday my heart flies harder trying to
Stay.
She's the only reason I'm still here.
As the minute passes,
My heart grows nearer,
Never quite knowing where he's at,
Never quite caring.
Just persevering,
To fly,
To fly and try,
Try to catch up to the one he wants.
His one desire.
Her scent fills him with the appetite of a
Fire.
And the story ends,
With her too far away.
My heart will never mend.

Sigh

Sometime I wonder why.
Why was I born so shy?
All I wish is I could tell her,
How I feel,
And how much I would care.
When I see her smile,
My heart becomes a blooming rose.
She the most beautiful thing,
That anyone has ever seen.

Simply Misty

She's all if ever think about,
She's the only thing ever on my mind,
She's in all my dreams,
But dreams are hard to find,
I wonder day to day,
Whether she still dreams of me,
I wonder every night,
Whether or not she still loves me,
I hope she does,
I even pray,
I dream of us together a long time from now,
The way I hope things turn out to be.
But I am a hopeless romantic,
Who thrives on misery?
I wish I could be happy,
But if know I can't be without her.
Her gorgeous smile, her warming touch,
Her beautiful eyes,
All of her great features,
I have pain living without.

Stolen Heart

I never knew what love was till I met her;
A passion started to grow in my heart;
Her beautiful eyes, gorgeous smile.
No one's ever been so beautiful to me.
A wish we were still together;
I'll love her forever;
The subject of all my dreams;
Swift flowing streams;
Nature's soothing sounds;
We're both lying on the ground;
Staring at the stars;
Holding her in my arms;
Never letting her go;
My heart she stole.

Stranger

Kindle of my fire;
Hairs a brown ash;
Lips a luscious red;
She's the one thing I desire;
The modern inconvenience of cash;
"Money is the root of all evil,"
Someone once said;
The greatest gift ever known;
Worth more than its weight in gold;
The protection from danger;
The aid of a complete stranger:
Who is he?
Why does he help you?
The answer to the questions;
Can be deep inside your heart;
But it's up to you to start.

Sunset

Cool wind in my hair;
Air tastes as sweet as a pear.
Watching the sun go down;
the trees shading a darker brown.
The sky's purple, orange, and red;
some people are just getting out of bed.
The most beautiful site you could ever see;
Wish you could've been there with me.
But that's the past;
Life goes by a little too fast.
So hold on tight;
and don't let the bedbugs bite.
A simple pleasure;
a moment to treasure.

Tear Me Apart

Pull my heart strings any further and they just might break.
Put me back in my place.
Hide me from your beautiful face.
Torment me with your presence,
It's not that if don't like it, I just love it.
And it's tearing me apart.
Does she even feel the same?
I'll pull through, if only if knew the truth.
She's tearing me apart... from the inside.
Its 4 A.M., and if haven't slept a wink.
I can't close my eyes...
If I do she'll be the only thing on my mind.
Please just make it stop...

Colors of a Rose

The red rose dreams passion;
The white rose dreams love.
The red rose a falcon;
The white rose a dove.

But I send you a flushed red, white rose bud,
For the love that is purest and sweetest,
Has a kiss of eternal bliss on the lips.

Lady of my Dreams

My dreams are of a lady,
Very dear to me.
I dream of us together forever,
The way I hope life turns out to be.
She is everything to me,
Most beautiful creature you'll ever see.
Her lips the most incredible shade of red.
It's impossible to get thoughts of her out of my head.
She is the lady of my dreams,
She means everything to me,
She's the water to my hearts tree.

The Nights Poem

Beautiful gallant night,
Filled of stars so bright,
Help me find my way home,
To which I have lost my way.
Show me the passage of time,
So I may judge my wine,
And have a large bounty,
Of which I may give to you,
The greatest fruits of mine.
Keep thou moon bright,
Let thou light grow,
Protect me from the shadow,
And give me thou strength,
So I may slay my fear,
And find my way home.

The Past

I feel alone this night,
Searching for an internal light.
I search round and round,
Still it couldn't be found.
Dark as the deepest sea,
Or is it just me?
I sit and I wonder why,
How come I'm always so shy?
Do my poems always rhyme?
Since the dawn of all time.
If you could change a man's heart,
How do you know where to start?

The Sinners

The time has come,
To confess thy sins,
To cast down upon thee!
The burning sword of Loki!
Flaming, Temperate Metal,
Scolding and melding to your skin!
The luminous flame engulfs thee!
The smell of fear surrounds you,
As you tremble in your boot!
Wondering Why?
What is it you did to deserve this?
What horrible atrocity have you committed?
Judgment day has been cast down upon thee!
To forever burn in an eternal darkness!
Your soul has been sold!
Your black heart stripped from your now lifeless body!
All you will ever feel now is
Pain!
Despair!
The innocent whom you corrupted
Now inhabit every inch of your mind!
Chasing you threw the fiery fields of hell!
Finally you escape into the abyss!
And you fall, and you fall, and you fall!
It never ends,
The fear has caught up to you!
Feel the evil entrap you,
Feel it crawl through your spine,

The feeling will never quit growing,
Not until you accept what you have become,
The inferno abyss has you,
There is no going back now,
Forever your soul is lost,
Wandering the highways of hell,
The fire burns,
Doesn't it?
Boiling blisters swell upon you,
The pain is almost unbearable,
You would rather die?
But you are already dead.
What hero will come and save you now?
Who will be so willing?
Why would anyone care?
You souls already dead.
There is no redemption for you,
You will never see paradise,
All you will ever see now,
Is the darkness that was once you?

Two Isles

Trapped between two isles,
Drowning in a sea of despair.
Deciding which isle to swim to,
Less I drown and not go anywhere.
Which do I want to live with more?
Which is likely to care?
Which is likely to welcome me more?
To not throw me off of her ocean shore?
Both isles I have known well before.
Graced their sandy shores.
I remember the first quite well,
We met on a cold rainy day.
Yet, she brought the sun with her somehow.
I did not implore much about her.
She kept her secrets, and I kept mine.
Beautiful snow-capped mountains.
She smelled of tropical flowers.
I left the isle within three months,
Or rather, she left me.
I never did know quite why.

I did not want to leave, so little I knew,
So much I wanted to learn.
I loved the isle never quite knowing why.
I paid the isle visits every now and then.
Never speaking of times gone by,
Or how it could have been.
Only listening, waiting, and thinking of how

It could be.
Wondering if she'll ever let me in her life once more.
Then I wonder of the other isle.
One I know a little more of.
We fell in love, before we ever met.
She welcomed me with a warm, beautiful beach.
Beyond the beach,
Fields of roses as far as the eye could see.
She kept me warm with her winds gentle embrace.
When I was too cold, her breeze changed form,
And kept my blood warm once more.

Again, I had to leave.
The isle was slowly sinking,
And would forever vanish beneath the oceans
Floor.
Again I did not want to leave.
She didn't want me to leave either,
But it was for the best,
At least that's what she thought.
Now I'm torn between two choices.
Which Isle to return to?
If for only a short time.
To the left,
An isle of majestic beauty and mystery.
To the right,
The vanishing Isle of Aphrodite,
Sure to join Atlantis within half a year or
Less.
Yet worth every second of her time left.

So I'm torn between two choices,
A question pondering mankind,
Since the dawn of time.
Confronted with a fork in the road,
Shall he go left?

Or shall he go right?
Less he choose the unseen option and go nowhere,
In which case I would drown in a sea of despair

Unseen Treasures

Night, Night, Not So Bright;
Come Again another Night;
Night So Scary, Night So Eerie;
Once Upon a Midnight Dreary;
Night So late, Night So Dark;
Woken By the Mid-Summers Lark;
Night Can Be Good, Night Can Be Bad;
But you'll always have someone, it's Your Dad!

Valor: Cantos I – IV

"Sun rising from the east,
Moon falling to the west,
The time has come to slay the beast,
You must do your best,
Our future depends on your victory,
And you must do it urgently,
Every minute we wither away,
our fathers slowly decay,
And some of us,
on the inside,
Never stop crying,
Our hearts have stopped flying,
You must keep the monster at bay,
Or a great price we will pay."

"I shall do my best sire,
I will hear my calling,
Do as thou desire,
For it is my theology,
That these times are indeed dire,
and call for extreme measure,
For you,
I light the fire,
Consider it a pleasure."

"Good luck my child,
Be diligent and insightful,
Or life might turn out to be a little too
wild,
To your heart you must be faithful,

Or thou will never succeed,
We shall forever be grateful,
Take with you this gallant steed,
Pay consideration to the silent whisper of
the nymph's trees,
for only they know what you truly need,
and only they can bring us all jubilee."

"I shall do as thou request,
Listen to the Nymph's music made.
Shall, however, I succeed at my quest.
There is a person I wish to serenade."

Valor (Canto III)
"The price is fair Sir Knight.
Tell me of this lady who has stolen your heart.
But do take flight,
you have a quest you must start."

"A beautiful angel from above,
her heavenly wings she does sow.
we fell deep in love,
several enchanting weeks ago.
We held each other closely,
dreaming of future stars.
Her eye looked so heavenly,
together, we dreamt of lands afar."

"Tell me of this girl you so deeply love.
What house is she of?
I shall speak to her lord."

"Dear sire, there will be no need for such.
For I have just spoken with her father,
and well he has told me of things dear and
dire,
And of a horrid beasts bother.
The quest he sought me out for will

transpire.
With all but a single agreement.
The taking of his daughters Marion's hand,
Gold to establish a settlement,
in some far away land."

"It pains me so,
to give my daughters hand away.
But if to thou it must go,
Make sure your heart never falls astray,
or a high price you will pay."

"My love for you daughter will never waver,
of this if swear,
She will always be my favor.
The terms are now fair,
it brings me great pleasure to start my
quest,
Now that you have promised me you're most
precious treasure."

What to Say

I met a girl the other day,
I didn't know quite what to say,
I thought about her for the rest of the day.
She was so fascinating to me,
most beautiful thing I've ever seen,
I hope someday she will be with me.

I tried to ask her out one day,
but things never go my way,
I just didn't know what to say.

All my life;
I've been waiting for you!

All my life;
I've been waiting for someone like you

Every time, I close my eyes,
I see her there, next to me,
And I still don't know what to say!

When I met you

Days go by too fast.
It's hard to remember what's first, and what's last.
Several days to remember,
Hopefully in December.
It pains me when she's not nearby.
The heart loses its desire to fly.
I've been hanging on by a limb.
This memory will never dim.
When we first met.
I was chewing on a mint.
I told her my name,
Held my hand out with no shame.
That long brown hair,
I couldn't help but to stare.
The hand declined,
I've always wondered why.
My memories have been in a stir,
The rest is just an unwanted blur.

Mary Sues Poem

Star light, Star Bright,
I wished upon a star tonight.
I wish I may, I wish I might.
I wish if could see you every night.
I live here alone, and all if can think
About is you.
Your touch, your lips, your smile, your kiss
I could never get enough of you.
But if would wait years for you if I had too.
I would do anything to hole you close,
Argue who loves who most.
I would do anything to make you smile,
Even if it involved letting you tickle me
For a while.
I love you with all my heart.
I love you with all my soul.
I love you more than I ever thought
Possible.

For Love I Once Fell

I once fell in love with a girl.
She was so beautiful to me.
I loved everything about her.
Every aspect, every feature.
She meant so much to me,
More than anyone else ever had.
I am still in love with a girl,
Who is so beautiful to me?
I still love everything about her.
Every aspect, every feature.
She still means the world to me,
More than anyone else does.
I will always love this girl.
She will always be beautiful to me.
I will always love everything about her.
Every aspect, every feature.
She will always mean a lot to me.
More than anyone else ever will.

No matter what anyone may say,
My heart will always feel this way.
I will always be in love,
With a girl name misty.
But she will always hate me,
For I mistake I didn't make.
Her own faults to blame,
But she would never believe me.
But I go on, knowing things will never be

Again.
I am happy still,
For as long as I live,
I know the truth,
And I know how it should end.

Simply Misty II

Every second of every day,
Night after night,
Day after day,
I can't stop thinking about you.
I miss so much about you.
I miss so much about us.
But that isn't why I'm writing you.
I'm writing to let you know,
how beautiful I think you are.
I'm writing to let you know,
despite all the time that has gone by,
I can't stop,
being in love with you.
I look at your picture every night,
Hoping and Praying,
to see you again someday,
the next day,
or any other day.

I could wait forever,
just to be with you,
Just to see your face, your smile.
Just to hear you laugh, your voice.

I could buy you roses, diamonds, and jewels,
some of which I will.
I could write you poems, songs, and long love letters,
which I do.
But none of those are as important to me,

as being able to say three little words,
I love you.

So I lie here

So I lie here, Not able to sleep.
Wondering if she truly loves me.
She says she does, But at times I wonder.
I treat her so well, but she thinks I get
mad at her. I never have. I treat her so
well, but she seems to like upsetting me.
I don't why. But I love her more than
anything. But a lot of the time I cry.
Because of her. Because I don't know if she
cares. And I do. I worry for her. Does she
worry for me? Does she even care? I hope and
I pray, that maybe someday she'll
understand. I'm not like most people. The
things I do, the things I say, even the
things I think. I can't ever stop thinking
about her. About what would happen to me
if I lost her? But then I wonder, does she
even want to be with me?

The Meaning of a Rose

Roses are for poets, artists, lovers, and
musicians.
True romantics by their creed.
A rose forms poet's poems.
A rose paints an artist's masterpiece.
A rose is sealed by a lovers kiss.
A rose is in a musician's soul.
When a poet sends a rose,
it is full of words for love and caring.
When an artist sends a rose,
it is full of serene beauty only an artist
can see,
when a lover sends a rose,
it is full of whispered sweet nothing, and tender kisses.
When a musician sends a rose,
It is full of melodic melodies wrote only for you.
When I send a rose,
it is full of all these and more.
For my love for you goes beyond words.
For my love for you goes past images.
For my love for you goes farther than a tender kiss.
For my love for you is my own sweet melody

While I Was Away

Every moment I was away,
I thought deeply of you,
Every day I was away,
thinking of you got me through,
But it didn't matter,
every day I was away,
you thought more of someone else,
it doesn't matter,
you'll always be
thinking of someone else.
No matter what I do,
how hard I try,
you'll always fall for
someone else.
I thought a kiss meant something,
but apparently it meant nothing.
Every moment of every day,
I thought about a kiss,
I thought about your lips,
I thought about you,
and those are the thoughts that pushed me through.
To the end,
I'll always think about you.
Whether or not you feel the same,
I always will,
I'll always care,
and in the end,
that's all that really matters.

With or Without You

With, or without you.
Forever Burning,
I yearn for my release,
from this imprisonment,
Of falsely spoken lies,
Burn with me,
These Lies of deceit,
I have lost my love,
And as such I have lost myself,
AS I burn in this fiery hell.
Torment ME! Torture ME!
Take my soul away!
Release me,
The pain is too much to bare,
Release me,
The bleeding isn't stopping,
Release me,
I can't take the torture any longer.
With or without you,
I only feel pain,
with or without you,
my heart tortures me.

Everything Changes

Running through life, and everything changes.
Running away and everything is changing.
So much has happened in such a short time
So many changes
In my life

How I wish things could be
The way they were
The days if Held you
The days you smiled over me
I could never forget
The brush of your lips
So many changes
Unwelcome changes

My life's gone through so many changes
In such a short while,
Unwelcome changes,
Unwelcome changes.

For Someone

Is it wrong for me to love you
Knowing so little about your life?
Maybe I'm just being foolish
for putting my heart through all this strife.

What I feel could not be mistaken
for lust or infatuation;
what I feel for you seems real,
and it brightens up every dull situation.

What if nothing ever comes of us,
And I never get to tell you how I feel?
What if I keep it all inside,
And I never get to know if my feelings are real?

All I know is every time I see you
I want to open up my heart,
for some reason I'm afraid
that nothing will ever start.

If I let you know how I feel
I don't want to look stupid
And see the look on your face
Asking me why I did what I did.

How I want so much to hold you
and feel your arms around me
telling me you feel the same
and together we could truly be.

I look into your sparkling eyes

and smile back at you
as we are about to kiss, the dream ends
I realize it's not true.

You could never feel that way for me
you could never look at me that way.
So before I go to bed at night
I kneel down and pray.

For a chance to get to know you
as a friend and hopefully more
as I grow to love you day by day
these dreams don't suffice like before.

I need more than dreams
I need you.
And I need to feel happy
I need this love to be true...

Break Apart the Silence

Break apart the Silence,
Break apart his heart,
Tell him you love him,
Then tear him apart,
I'm not the enemy,
I'm not your adversary,
I can see through you,
I am not the enemy,
I see you belief,
Now Face Him,
All His Desires,
Tell him Lies,
To Make Him Alright,
Untrue To Him,
As He Lays Awake At Night,

Dreams he has of you,
Keep him alive,
Tell him you love him,
So he can hold his head high,
Tell him you love him,
But don't tell him a lie,

Feel the Blackness

Why did you leave me?
What did I do?
I always loved you,
No matter what we went through.
Now you have left me,
and I don't think I'll make it through,
Tomorrow is empty,
if I can't be with you.

 I feel the blackness,
as my tears are falling,
I can't hold them back.
I feel the blackness,
my soul is dying,
waiting for you to come back,

Tell me the truth now,
I never lied to you,
I've always been honest,
Why'd you put me through,
this maze of broken hearts.
Look what you started,
See what I've become.
Heart covered darkness

I'm in Love with Suicide

Love struck,
or just by Dumb Luck,
All for you,
I fell over the edge,
dreaming of you.
I fell
Hold me back,
from this ledge,
Hold me back,
from you.
Lost
I've become,
in your world of hate
and mistrust,
Lost,
I can't be found.

Feel
the pain
As they pull
my strings
Tied
to my heart,
Tied
to you,

Every day,
I think of jumping,
I want to die,

Just for you,

Ever day,
I feel like dyeing,
Almost Every day,
I feel like dyeing,
Just hold me back,
please hold me back,

Feel my pain,
It hurts so much,
Inside you,
I desire.
To be with you,
I can't go on
No longer,

Love Sober

Breaking every promise made,
her trust falls short of me.
I am everything she wants,
I am everything she needs.
I just want to start things over,
I just want us to be together,
why not now,
why not forever.

My dreams cannot be held forever,
My heart's become love sober,
My souls about to break,
because of you my heart aches

Take me heart away
I gave it all to you,
tell me why it hurts
tell me what to do
I loved you endlessly
I held you close at night
now why must I hurt
now why must I fight,

So you've come to a dead end
and you don't know what to do,
running circles around in your head,
thinking of a way through.
To get you back,

STEVEN MCCOMBS

with me to stay,
for all my life,
to never stray,

And now I'm love sober.....

Loving you is so hard

Pulling my heart out from inside of me.
I can't help but to bleed.
Breaking every vain inside of me.
I can't seem to stop the screaming.
And it won't go away, until I'm dead.
It won't go away, until I'm dead.
Listening to all the words you say.
Leave your lies out of my way.
I don't need your pain,
my dreams will pray for me.
An I don't need your pain,
my dream will pray for me.

I want to feel your love again.
I want to feel your love again.
I want to feel your kiss upon my skin.
I need to feel your love again.
I need to feel your love again.
I need to see your face.
I need you loving embrace.
I need to feel you love again.
Loving you is so hard.
When you love someone else.
My heart will stay with you.
Until the end of time.
I miss you so much.
I forgot how much it hurts, to be alone.
I feel like I am dying.
Whenever I'm without you.

I can't stop crying.
Ohhhh
While I'm thinking about you
I keep on crying.
I want to feel your love again.
I want to feel your love again.
I want to feel your kiss upon my skin.
I need to feel your love again.
I need to feel your love again.
I need to see your face.
I need you loving embrace.
I need to feel your love again.

Loving you is so hard when you love someone else....
Loving you is so hard when you don't love me...
Loving you is so hard when you love someone else.
Loving you is so hard when you don't love me...

Walls

Do you understand
what if mean
when if say
I love you?
Tell me what you want,
tell me how to love you.
There is no truth in love,
it's all a shamble of lies.
There is no truth in love,
it all leads to painful lives.
I don't want to feel this way.
Don't want to feel the walls close upon me.
Feel my heart turn to stone.
Hear it fall through my soul.
Drowning in a sea on loneliness,
tell me what our future holds.
Why can't you see,
what you mean to me?
How could you break my heart,
and then break me?
I thought you loved me,
Really cared about me,
I thought you finally saw clearly,
The love that we had.
I thought you'd never leave me,
to save me,
to leave me here so sad.
If thought you'd understand

that I love you.
Feel the walls,(close upon me)
Feel the walls close upon me,(upon me)
Feel the walls,(close upon me)
Feel the walls as my heart engulfs me.
68

Addict

I can't fight it;
I can't deny it;
When my heart is breaking with every word, that you speak.
I can't take it;
the pressure,
that is flowing through my veins about to break.

I Need
So much
To feel you by my side.
I need you
So much

I've never felt this way about anyone but you,
I've never felt this way.
I've never felt this way about anyone but you,
I've finally realized,
Love's perfect in my eye.

This pain;
Consume me;
I lost my soul as you cam lurching,
Through my heart
Pathetic,
Little junkie,
I'm the whore that needs you one more time
Perfect in my eye

You're perfect in my eye

This is my Holiday

I've been waiting for this holiday,
But you've been taking things so seriously,
I just want to relax,
I just want to have fun,
I just want to hold you before this day is done.
I'm laughing out loud,
you're laughing to,
Thinking of all that we've been through.
I just want to hold you,
And tell the truth,
It 4 AM, I should be in bed,
But if can't get you out of my head,
But if can't take it anymore,
I just want to let you know,
things are over with me an you.

I saw you with that other guy,
I saw you kissing him last night,
I was hoping you were the one,
But now my hoping is done,
Cuss your just another slut.

You said it would be the one,
But now things are undone,
you said he was just a friend,
you forgot to mention you were together in bed.

Roll the Dice

The wheel spins around and around,
will you choose the right one
fall into the game
you're being played
the pawn, the rook, or the king, the queen,
none of it matters,
you're going to lose anyway,
roll the dice,
go back five spaces,
roll the dice,
it's the game of life,
a game of chance,
rigged so you can't win,
motifs and alibies,
are all you really need,
take you chance,
roll the dice.
The well spins round and around.
The wheel spin around again.

Another Love Poem

You remind me of a girl,
Who's never been wrote a poem.

You remind me of a girl,
Who's never been given a rose?

It makes no sense to me,
You're mind makes its own brand of poetry.
You're body reminds me of its own beautiful rose.

You are said to have loved many.
But among them I doubt there ever was a poet.

For if you were my rose,
I would hold you gently as I caressed you're fragile skin.

If you were my rose,
I would whisper reassuring words of sweetness and love into
you're rose buds.
I would do these things for hours.

A poet can teach you things you never knew.
They open your mind, and open your heart.

If I could be anything for anyone,
I would be anything only for you.

For you are my only rose.
You are my only love.

Just another Love Song

Just another Day,
Just another broken heart.
We've haven't been together long,
but already, if feel you tearing at my heart,
This isn't fair
I fall for you
an you torment me

we can have a live to share,
to mend these wounds,
if only you cared,
you make me promises,
but you never follow through,

this is how things have fallen apart before,
I don't want it to happen,
I won't let it happen.
I want you to know I care,
I want you to know if love you.

But sometimes if feel like you aren't listening.
Another day goes by, and if ask myself if you know the way
if feel about you.

And if can't be in your arms,
I'll try my best to be next to you,
but always if wonder if you want me there.

Show Me How

Don't you know,
I can't live without you,
My nightmare has become whole,
Living without you,
Sleeping,
You're there,
Drug me up,
With your kiss,
I thought I could make it,
Without you,
I was such a fool,
To think I wouldn't stumble,
Poisoned,
Your there,

Cold and angry,
Sleep and agony,
Fill me,

Heaven help me,
Heavens creation helps me pray,
Allow me to forget,
Show me how to forget you,
So I can let go

And I breathe…
And I breathe…
And I breathe…
I can't breathe without you

Sweet Sweet Innocence

Sweet sweet innocence
Where have you gone
You were an angel
Waiting for me
But now I have lost you
Where have you gone

Tender bliss
From you luscious kiss
I miss your love
I miss your kiss
Sweet sweet angel
Just in case
I don't come home
May I have another kiss.

Thrill Kill

I feel,
Full of hate,
I want,
To tear you apart,
I need,
To break you,

Tell me,
What's going on?
Tell me,
No leave me alone,
I don't want to see you either.

For only a matter of instance,
I was with you,
for only an iota of time,
I was next to you,
why does it always end up like this...?

Kill me....
Thrill me...
Tell me your thoughts,

Thrill me...
Kill me....
I Need your Love

I ended up in a black hole,
Staring through the void,
I ended up dyeing,

In my nightmare.

Why weren't you there to save me?
Do you even truly care?
About me.

Aghhhhhhhhhhhhhhhhhhhhhhhh!!!!
Tell me
Aghhhhhhhhhhhhhhhhhhhhhhhhh!!!!
Tell me

Sometimes I feel like I'm dying,
When I can't be near you,
Sometimes I feel like crying,
When I talk to you,

Kill me....
Thrill me...
Tell me your thoughts,

Thrill me...
Kill me....
I Need your Love

Kill me....
Thrill me...
Tell me your thoughts,

Thrill me...
Kill me....
I Need your Love

Empty me,
Of this void,
Fill me,
Of your love again,

Feel the pressure,
As it wounds me slowly,

Feel my heart ache,
As it goes on without you...

Sometimes I feel like crying,
when I talk to you,

kill me....
Thrill me...
Tell me your thoughts,

Thrill me...
Kill me....
I Need your Love

Kill me....
Thrill me...
Tell me your thoughts,

Thrill me...
Kill me....
I need your Love

Empty me,
of this void,
Fill me,
of your love again.

Break

I want to break
I want to tear you apart
Stupid mother fuckers
I'm going to rip you apart
Tear and chew
And rip you apart
Tear and chew
And pull out your heart

Blood blood sweat
Watch me bleed
Blood blood sweat
Begging please
It won't stop
The pain
The red
Come to me
Make me bleed
Tear me apart
Begging please
What the fuck is going on
What the fuck is taking so long

Ecstasy and empathy
Ecstasy and empathy
Bring it to me

I want to break
I want to tear you apart.

Trembling

I woke up this morning,
From luscious dreams of you,
All I could think of all night,
Is the shit I put up with from you,

Trembling my skin flows for you,
Crumbling my heart goes because of you,
Tumbling I go without you.

I never did anything wrong to you,
I did everything I could for you,
Still I come tumbling down without you.

My soul, it burns without you…
My Heart, Can't live without you….
So I go, on without you….
So I go, living without you….

Broken Glass Jar

If I'd only tired a little harder,
Maybe we would still be together.

 I feel so alone!
 As the darkness surrounds me.
I feel so desperate!
As my heart rejects the pain.
I feel so wasted!
As if my life means nothing

I miss your laugh, I miss your kisses.
One star, I've made so many wishes.
Take this glass jar of loneliness away from me
I don't want it anymore.
Fill me again of hope,
please tell me you once loved me!

I'd almost given up on life.
I believed in nothing.
Then I met you.
You're everything to me.
Please don't throw my love away.
Take this jar of loneliness away from me,
I don't want it anymore!!

every time that I see you,
I feel so far away.
Why can't things be,

just like they used to be?

Everything used to be perfect, (perfect)
and then you left me........
Please take away this emptiness that haunts me,
I don't want this Glass jar of loneliness anymore.

Wake Up

I fall asleep
so I can see you
within my own false reality.
I fall asleep
so I can be with you
in my false reality
in my dreams
you love me
but in reality
that will never be.
Wake me up from this false reality,
show me what is real.
I am the one that was meant for you,
tell me what to do.
I'll love you forever
until the day I die.

Wake me up so I can feel, (So I can feel)
That the world around me is real,
That all this is an illusion
That my dreams have lied to me,
You're the lady of my dreams.
But in reality it will never be.

why can't you just see?
That I want you here with me!
I can't stop thinking about you,
don't know what I would do without you.
Wondering when you'll be here,

Wondering when you'll stand near,
to me.
I go to bed every night,
Thinking of the things that I've done wrong,
trying to figure out,
how to get a hold of you heart.
You mean all the world to me,
and yet you still cannot see,
the love I feel for you.

I don't want to wake
from these dream I have of you.
I don't want to wake
from the memories I have of you.
Wake up, (wake up)
Wake up, (wake up)
Wake up and see my false realities.

and now I can see clearly............

What will you do now?

What will you do now?
That you've thrown us away?
What will you do now?
That everything's been broken by you?
Why'd you do this to me?

Love hurts,
And kills believes,
This is what you've done to me,
And this is what you've done for me,
You've done nothing for me,
You've done nothing,
You've done nothing for me,
You've done nothing.

Why do you tell me?
All these things I don't want to know,
why do you tell me?
All of these things about you,
why do you do this to me?

Love hurts,
And kills believes,
This is what you've done to me,
And this is what you've done for me,
You've done nothing for me,
You've done nothing,
You've done nothing for me,

You've done nothing.

You've done nothing for me,
You've done nothing,
You've done nothing for me,
You've done nothing,
You've done nothing for me,
You've done nothing,

Love hurts,
And kills believes,
This is what you've done to me,
And this is what you've done for me,
You've done nothing for me,
You've done nothing,
You've done nothing for me,
You've done nothing.

Love hurts,
And kills believes,
This is what you've done to me,
And this is what you've done for me,
You've done nothing for me,
You've done nothing,
You've done nothing for me,
You've done nothing.
You've done nothing for me,
you've done nothing.
You've done nothing for me,
you've done nothing.
You've done nothing for me,
you've done nothing.
You've done nothing for me.

I'll turn you around

I want your touch,
I Need your lips
I want your love,
I need your kiss.
I'm everything you need,
just wait and see.
A Better love,
you'll never know.
Baby you need me.

I can turn your life around,
be the best time of our lives.
As our hearts start beating faster and faster,
You begin to undress,
As I feel you're caress,
Thoughts are screaming in my head,
as we get out of bed,
Baby, It's all that we needed..

Our touch, our kiss, our love,
Will turn things around.

Midnight Thoughts

You lift my heart above the clouds whenever if see you, hear your
voice,
or touch you,
but every minute
imp away from you,
thoughts of you and
what if can't have make me miserable.

Spending any time with you,
you're so beautiful,
and unattainable.
Difficulty,
Makes me want you more

Dreaming of you,
Makes me miserable.
Knowing you want it too,
Holding, Caressing, Kissing, and Loving.

Where will we be,
Years from now.
Where should we be?
All I know,
Is if want to be in your arms,
Tonight,
years from tonight.
Holding you, and loving you.

Your Kiss is all that I Need

I want your touch,
I Need your lips
I want your love,
I need your kiss.
I'm everything you need,
just wait and see.
A Better love,
you'll never know.
Baby you need me.

I can turn your life around,
be the best time of our lives.
As our hearts start beating faster and faster,
You begin to undress,
As I feel you're caress,
Thoughts are screaming in my head,
as we get out of bed,
Baby, It all that we needed..

Just another Song for you

I wrote a song for you,
but you aren't listening.
I wrote a song for your,
but you don't care.

What do you know of me?
I am suffering,
from these lies you tell me.

Even if could read your mind,
you, would lie to me.

I will not suffer,
If can help it.
I will not suffer

Tears overwhelm my nights,
well dreaming of you,
I can't help it,
but you don't care.
Stabbing my broken heart.
Peeling an open wound.

Crushing on you

I'm crushing on you,
and if don't know why.
It may be your pretty eyes,
Beautiful smile,
or those sexy thighs.
Whenever if think about you,
I drive myself wild.
I can't help it.
I don't know why.
I can't get you out of my mind.
You're so beautiful,
I can't stop thinking of you.
Your lips, my lips.
And a Kiss.

I have to let you know

Every second of every day,
Night after night,
Day after day,
I can't stop thinking of you.

I Miss so much about you,
I miss so much about us.
But that isn't why I'm writing to you.

I'm writing to let you know,
how beautiful you are,
more than any nights star.
I'm writing to let you know,
Despite all the time that's gone by,
I just can't stop,
Being in love with you.

I look at your picture every night,
Hoping and praying,
to see you again someday.
The next day,
or any other day.

I could wait forever just to be with you,
Just to see your face, your smile,
Just to hear your laugh, to hear your voice.

I could buy you roses, diamonds, and jewels,
someday I probably will.
I could write you poems, song, and long love letters,
all of which if do,

STEVEN MCCOMBS

But none of those are as important to me
as three little words that mean everything
I love you.

Does She?

I lay here and wonder,
The answer to a question that is hard to ask;
Does she love me? Does she care?
A question that can't be answered by a single word,
Only by their actions.
Thinking about the answer pains me,
I've never loved someone so much,
I would do anything for her,
Climb the highest mountain
Swim the deepest sea,
I would turn the stars around for her,
I'd find a way somehow.
I'd never let my love go,
Not now, or ever.

Haikus

SLOW DEATH

Pale Ashen wood
Enveloped by gold flowers,
Fading, Gradually.

FREEDOM

Minute, White flower,
entangled, within the earth,
release they await.

THE WASP

clear, blue sky above
dark, open meadows below,
jet black wasp a flight

HOME

red, burning sunlight
shimmering thread confusing
eight legged creature

THE FRUIT

sapphire, jeweled birds,
gliding to the emerald tree,
dine on red, berries.

Can't Help Myself

Sometimes I feel like I am alone,
like there is no one around.
Sometime I feel like somebody else,
And I can't Help it.
I feel alone without you,
I Don't want you to leave me,
Like they have all left me.
I don't need it,
to feel so alone,
and I can't help myself.

Living here without you,
if only you were here.
I don't want anything else,
and I can't help myself,
wishing you were here.

Sometime I hurt myself,
as thoughts of you creep through my mind,
this dream, will last forever.

In the dream,
I was with you,
your beautiful eyes,
as we lay naked on the floor,
hearts beating,
Feeling your gentle embrace.
Feeling your kiss,
upon my lips.

The Pleasure inside You

Wasting my time......
I lost everything......
My feelings fade away......
As I fall farther from you.....
I don't know...
How to please you,
And I don't Know,
That I need you to myself,
And I'm selfish,
I try to please you,
And I don't know,
Anything anymore.......

Fading memories of us...
I never thought that...
We would end like this....
I have tried so hard...
To keep things the same...

And I don't know,
anything anymore.

Breath

I fall endlessly into the pool of her eyes,
not knowing if the motion will ever end,
not wanting to stop.
Only wanting to feel,
the taste of her lips.
The tenderness of a possible kiss.
Breathe

Moments

Every moment of every day,
You are all I ever think about,
At night, you are all I ever dream about,
To my friends, you are all I ever speak about.
I don't know why,
but my heart has always belonged to you,
And no matter what happens,
it always will.
I love you,
my heart tells me you love me too.
I've missed you so much,
my heart tells me you have missed me too.
I wish I knew what I had to do.
I suppose I can only wait for you,
It is what I want to do.
Because all I want is you.
All I need is you.
Without you,
I have been a wreck.
I don't want to go through that mess again.
I've wrote you so many letter,
So many poems,
You'll probably never see most of them,
I don't even know if I will, or if I should
Give you this one.
But I know...
Without a shadow of a doubt,
That I, am deeply in love,

With a woman who brightens my day whenever I see her,
A woman, who is one of the best parents I know,
A woman, who is charming and beautiful,
A woman, who's simple voice calms and strengthens me
For these things I thank you.
I wish I had a rose,
to sneak in your pocket with this note.
I promise you, I will buy you flowers again soon,
I find you so beautiful,
And I just want you to truly know,
I Love you,
In more way then I could ever truly tell you,
But that won't stop me from trying.

I am not a Poet

Who am I?
What does it matter, why do you care?
Are you going to fix my problems?
Perhaps take me away from here?
I will indulge you, perhaps perplex you.
For I, am not a Poet,
And this you will not believe
A Poet writes,
about the beautiful falling sunsets of autumn.
About love conquering the world,
about true romance, and struggles of happiness.
I am not a Poet.
I am Poetry
but that is not all,
what else am I?
Many more things, and many less.
A friend, a lover,
A son, a Soldier,
The list goes on and on,
But only one thing is important.
I am not a Poet
I AM POETRY
living to conquer this strange world of love,
breathing of romance and happiness
bringing with me, the warm glow of an autumn sunset.
I am poetry.

Evergreen Terrace

There was once a place if used to go,
where the roses grew,
and the birds flew,
the grass was green,
the water a crystalline gleam.
But that place has gone away
filled with a void,
black, and dark, and empty.
Lies, and deceit.
From those who have been corrupted, they are fools.
Who follow a blind path,
led by a woman,
tempting, and luring.
She is misleading.
Her voice,
that of a siren,
temptress of the sea.
Seduce me.
Reality is no more.
There is only her, my lady, my siren.
More Beautiful than the sea.

Remembrance

The days will come,
The days will go,
But every day we will remember,
The faith and the hope you brought unto us,
I look around me
And see the sorrow,
As my heart flies with hopes of tomorrow,
And every other day that will go bye,
I think of your lost life,
Wondering if it will ever happen to me.
You think well you're young, you're invincible
That nothing will ever happen to you,
Gambling with your life,
I wonder to myself why?
Things are so confusing to me right now.
Why does god end a good life?

Dancing the Stars Away

I want to wake up wherever you are,
lying next to you and kissing you gently.
I want to go wherever you go.
Holding your hand,
and romantically dancing.

I want to see what your eyes see.
Beauty and wonder getting lost in each other.
This is me,
who I want to be,
with you by my side,
Forever and ever.

Someday it will be,
you and me.
Forever and ever,
dancing the stars away.
Someday it will be,
you and me.
Forever and ever
Dancing the stars away.

I want to wake up every morning next to you,
tell you that you are beautiful.
You may be So very far away,
In my heart,
You'll always be by my side,
Lost in these feelings I've never been so happy,
And I've never been so scarred.

I don't want to lose you,
It's happened before,
and I'm afraid,
I'll mess up somewhere.

Someday it will be,
you and me.
Forever and ever,
dancing the stars away.
Someday it will be,
you and me.
Forever and ever,
 Dancing the stars away.

Loving You Is So Hard

Pulling my heart out from inside of me.
I can't help but to bleed.
Breaking every vain inside of me.
I can't seem to stop the screaming.
And it won't go away, until I'm dead.
It won't go away, until I'm dead.
Listening to all the words you say.
Leave your lies out of my way.
I don't need your pain,
my dreams will pray for me.
I don't need your pain,
my dream will pray for me.

I want to feel your love again.
I want to feel your love again.
I want to feel your kiss upon my skin.
I need to feel your love again.
I need to feel your love again.
I need to see your face.
I need you loving embrace.
I need to feel you love again.

Loving You is so hard.
When you love someone else.
My heart will stay with you.
Until the end of time.
I miss you so much.

I forgot how much it hurts, to be alone.
I feel like I am dying.
Whenever I'm without you.
I can't stop crying.
Ohhhh
While I'm thinking about you
I keep on crying.
Yeahhahh

I want to feel your love again.
I want to feel your love again.
I want to feel your kiss upon my skin.
I need to feel your love again.
I need to feel your love again.
I need to see your face.
I need you loving embrace.
I need to feel your love again.

Loving you is so hard when you love someone else....
Loving you is so hard when you don't love me…
Loving you is so hard when you love someone else.
Loving you is so hard when you don't love me

Sweet Fire

Let me tell you a story....
I've never felt this way before,
From the Moment,
I first saw you,
You stole my heart out the door.
This feelings,
Like Fire,
Sweet Fire,
I must have more
Picnics by starlight,
Romance by candlelight.
Lakeside twilight.
This feelings,
Like Fire,
Sweet Fire,
I hope you feel it too.
Your smiles a thousand different shades of sunlight,
Your brown eyes sparkle like millions of stars in the moonlight,
You're an Inspiration,
An out of this world sensation.
Janel,
You're amazingly wonderful,
In all the right ways
I want to kiss and hold you,
Till the end of our days.
I want to cross oceans with you,
Would climb the highest of mountains for you,
I want to see the world with you,
Together there is nothing we can't do.

STEVEN MCCOMBS

These feelings like fire,
Sweet fire,
These Feelings Like fire,
Sweet fire,
And I've fallen in love with you.

About The Author

Steven Mccombs

Steven McCombs has been writing poetry since he was 10. He currently resides in Las Vegas Nevada with his dog Alfie. His hobbies include Roller Derby, Swing Dancing, Painting, Table Top Gaming, Board Gaming, and Video Gaming. He also has a YouTube channel and will occasionally stream on twitch.